CHEESE

Illustrations by Melissa Sweet

CHRONICLE BOOKS

SAN FRANCISCO

QUICK AND EASY RECIPES FOR ELEGANT ENTERTAINING

CHEESE

By Lou Seibert Pappas

ACKNOWLEDGMENTS

With many thanks to cheese buyer Andrea London of Draeger's Supermarkets for her expertise on cheese, and to Betsy Clebesch and Cathie Colson for recipe lore. Again, Carolyn Miller proved an invaluable editor.

Text and recipes copyright © 1996 by Lou Seibert Pappas.
Illustrations copyright © 1996 by Melissa Sweet. All rights reserved.
No part of this book may be reproduced in any form without written permission from the publisher.

Pappas, Lou Seibert.
   Cheese: quick and easy recipes for elegant entertaining / by Lou Seibert Pappas; illustrated by Melissa Sweet.
     p. cm.
   Includes index.
   ISBN 0-8118-0814-9
   1. Cookery (Cheese) 2. Cheese. 3. Entertaining. I. Title.
   TX759.5.C48P37 1996   95-21498
   641.6'73--dc20   CIP

Printed in Hong Kong.
Book and jacket design by Pamela Geismar and Casey Reas.

Distributed in Canada by Raincoast Books, 8680 Cambie St., Vancouver, B.C. V6P 6M9

10 9 8 7 6 5 4 3 2 1

Chronicle Books
275 Fifth Street
San Francisco, CA 94103

CONTENTS

INTRODUCTION

It seems miraculous that more than two thousand kinds of cheese are made just from milk, plus a few natural additives. This process has been going on for centuries; in fact, the ancient Greeks believed that cheese was a gift from the gods.

Its myriad forms and countless varieties make cheese a sophisticated staple and a connoisseur's delight. One of the most nutritious and satisfying of foods, cheese is prized and savored for its high levels of protein and calcium, its keeping qualities, and its wide range of flavors, textures, and aromas.

HOW CHEESE IS MADE

The basic cheese-making process is simple: Milk is coagulated into soft, white curds and whey, the remaining thin liquid. Most cheeses are made from the curd, but a few are made from the whey. Any mammal's milk—cows, sheep, goats, water buffalo, and even yaks, camels, and reindeer—can be made into cheese. The milk may be whole or skim, or cream may be added. The higher the fat content, the creamier and smoother the final cheese.

Cheese may be made from either pasteurized or raw (unpasteurized) milk. Pasteurizing kills bacteria that impart unique flavors to cheese, yet raw-milk cheeses are also potential carriers of disease-causing bacteria. Both imported and domestic raw-milk cheeses must be aged at least sixty days to be sold in this country; by then the natural enzymes that age the cheese also kill any harmful bacteria. Fresh raw-milk cheeses are available to travelers in other countries, particularly France; caution should be taken in eating them due to the potential danger of illness.

Typically, milk to be made into cheese is heated between 70° and 100°F and lactic acid, calf rennet, or plant rennet is added, causing the mixture to curdle. The whey is then drained, and the curds are cut, molded, pressed, kneaded, or stretched. Some cheeses are eaten absolutely fresh, while most others are ripened for varying lengths of time. Cheeses in this category may be exposed to bacteria in order to help ripen them. A host of factors affect the final product: the climate, the environment, the source of the milk, the curing process, the additives, and the length of ripening time.

TYPES OF CHEESE

Classifying cheese can be complex, as many categories overlap because of differences in texture and ripening techniques. For simplicity, cheeses divided here fall into two basic groups:

Fresh, unripened or natural cheeses: These are made by a coagulating process using gentle heat or lactic acid; home recipes may use lemon juice. Types include cottage cheese, ricotta, feta, farmer's cheese, cream cheese, and Neufchâtel.

Ripened cheeses: These are made from curds created by the action of rennet. The amount of moisture left in the curds determines the eventual texture of the cheese, whether soft like Brie or Camembert, semifirm like Cheddar and Gruyère, or hard like Parmesan and Asiago. The ripened category includes blue, soft-ripened, washed-rind, Cheddar type, *grana*, Holland type, Swiss type, *pasta filata*, and goats' and sheeps' milk cheeses.

Blue cheeses develop from the inside out and include Danish Blue Castello, Oregon and Maytag Blue, Danablu, Cambozola, and Bleu de Bresse. Soft ripened cheeses ripen from the rind inward; when brought to room temperature they actually ooze, yet should never be liquid. Their edible rind may be powdery white or orange-hued. Goat and sheep cheeses may also be found in the first category. Grating, or *grana*, cheeses include Asiago, Parmesan, and dry jack.

Processed cheese is made by remolding pasteurized and reblended cheeses with certain additives. Because these cheeses have been altered in their production they lack the flavor and texture of natural cheese. Often water is added, and most have extra preservatives other than salt, often making them very high in sodium.

Low-fat and low-salt cheeses are proliferating today due to the trend toward healthful dining. Salt and fat create flavor in cheese. As the fat content decreases, cheeses become firmer in texture and less flavorful. Many low-fat cheeses have had more salt added to maintain flavor.

BUYING AND STORING

Appearance provides one of the best guides when buying any cheese. Buy from a reputable store with a high turnover.

Soft, fresh cheeses are highly perishable and should be kept tightly sealed in the refrigerator and eaten as quickly as possible. The harder the cheese, the less perishable it is. Wrap cheese tightly in plastic wrap or aluminum foil to seal out moisture, then slip into another sealed plastic bag or container and store away from foods with strong odors. For short storage for daily snacking, a crisper is a good location. For longer storage, the coldest area, in the back of the refrigerator, is best. Store blue cheeses separately from others, especially Cheddars. If mold has penetrated the cheese, simply cut the mold away.

Freezing cheese changes the texture and affects both flavor and aroma. If you have a surplus of cheese and must freeze it, hard cheeses will freeze more satisfactorily than soft cheeses. Cheddar types, well wrapped in foil and plastic wrap, can be frozen for up to 6 months. Creamy cheeses, such as blue cheeses, can be frozen but will become crumbly. Soft cheeses such as Brie can be frozen for a short time. Thaw cheese slowly in the refrigerator for 24 hours before using. Previously frozen cheeses are best used for cooking.

SERVING AND CUTTING

Except for cottage cheese, all cheese should be served at room temperature. If the weather is hot, the cheese will need to sit at room temperature for only half an hour; in warm weather, an hour may suffice; otherwise, allow 2 to 3 hours. Soft cheeses need a little less time to come to room temperature than do firm cheeses.

Tools for cutting cheese include spreaders, serrated knives, paddle-shaped slicers, wire cutters, cheese planers, triangular blades, double-handled knives, and cheese knives.

COOKING

Use low temperatures and short cooking times when cooking with cheese. Overcooking causes cheese to become tough and stringy, and the fat may separate out. (Processed cheese is an exception, as it melts readily into a creamy mass.) When substituting one cheese for another, select one with a similar flavor and texture.

ENTERTAINING WITH CHEESES

SELECTING A CHEESE TRAY

For a cocktail buffet party or a gala sit-down dinner, a cheese board with a selection of three or four cheeses is apropos. The aim is to choose a variety of flavors and textures. For an occasion when dinner will not be served and cheese stars, allow about 4 ounces of cheese per person. When dinner is to be served, allow about 1½ ounces for the cheese appetizer tray. Or, serve a selection of cheeses in the French way, as a separate cheese course that comes after the main course and before or instead of dessert.

For a pleasing, balanced selection of cheeses, choose three or four from among several types: a soft-ripened cheese such as Brie or Camembert; a blue cheese such as Gorgonzola or Roquefort; a goat cheese such as a French Montrachet or Saint-Maure; a firm cheese such as a farmhouse Cheddar or an Emmentaler; a hard cheese such as a Parmigiano Reggiano or a dry Monterey jack; and a double- or triple-cream cheese such as a Boursin or Saint-André.

TWO DOZEN CHEESES

Classifying cheeses presents a challenge. Fresh and ripened cheeses may be further divided by texture, by cheesemaking method, or the source of their milk: cow, sheep, goat, or water buffalo. They may be firm (such as Parmesan and Pecorino), semifirm (Cheddar and Jarlsberg), or semisoft (Edam and Monterey jack). Other categories include soft-ripened (like Brie or Camembert); washed-rind, or monastery type (Pont l'Évêque); double or triple cream (such as Boursin and Explorateur); blue (such as Gorgonzola or Stilton); *pasta filata*, meaning "spun curd" (such as mozzarella or provolone); brine-cured (such as feta); and whey type (Italian ricotta).

Among the thousands of cheeses in the marketplace, we have singled out two dozen of the most popular and available ones to profile in brief detail. Virtually all of these are made in the United States.

BRIE: One of the most famous and most imitated of all French cheeses, Brie dates back to the fifth century A.D. and was a favorite of Emperor Charlemagne in the eighth century. Made from pasteurized or unpasteurized cow's milk, it is characterized by a downy white bloom, or rind, and a cream-colored buttery interior that oozes when ripe. Select a plump and resilient Brie for a dessert tray or appetizer. A perfectly ripe Brie has a mushroom aroma and flavor.

CAMEMBERT: A renowned Normandy cheese, this cows' milk cheese has a white downy rind and creamy interior. When this cheese is tucked into its wooden box for aging, it has a thick, furry white bloom that looks like snow. By market time, the fuzz has dried and hardened to the familiar white crust. Camembert is now made in enormous quantities in virtually every European country and the United States. Napoleon III is credited with christening this cheese, naming it after the Norman village where it was served to him by Marie Harel, a farmer's wife and the daughter of the creator of the cheese. Camembert and water biscuits are a classic dessert duo.

CHEDDAR: The most widely made cheese in the world today originated in the village of Cheddar near Somerset, England. A firm cows' milk cheese, it varies in color from its natural white to a pumpkin orange, and in flavor from mild when young to mellow and nutty when mature; its quality also differs markedly. Most farmhouse and some commercial Cheddars are white. Orange Cheddar can be natural or artificially colored with annatto or other natural colorings. Cheddar is highly versatile for both snacking and cooking. Farmhouse Cheddars are still made in England's West Country and rank among the finest in the world. Mature American and Canadian Cheddars tend to be much sharper and are sometimes aged longer. Some of the finest American Cheddars come from Vermont and New York and are naturally white. As a rule, Vermont Cheddars are more mellow and moist than those as old from New York and Canada. Because New York Cheddars are aged in very dry curing rooms, they are crumblier than other cheeses and good for grating. Wisconsin and Oregon are known for Cheddars, and theirs are generally colored and aged less.

EDAM: Its spherical shape and shiny red paraffin seal make this cheese instantly recognizable, although in Holland Edam is sold with the natural golden rind uncovered. Made from part skim milk, there is a slightly acid aftertaste to its mellow flavor. An excellent all-purpose cheese, Edam is also a natural with beer.

EMMENTALER: The original "Swiss cheese," Emmentaler is Switzerland's oldest and most important cheese. This cows' milk cheese has marble-sized holes and a light gold color. It is exported in giant wheels, weighing from 150 to 220 pounds. The nutty-sweet, mellow flavor of Emmentaler makes it ideal for snacks, sandwiches, and fruit and cheese plates.

FETA: This sharp, salty white cheese is traditionally made in Greece from sheeps' or goats' milk; elsewhere producers use cows' milk. Crumbly and rindless, feta is usually pressed into square cakes and cured and stored in its own salty whey. It makes a zestful addition to salads and pita sandwiches.

FONTINA: Genuine Italian Fontina comes only from the Val d'Aosta, high up in the Alps near the Swiss and French borders. It has a creamy texture, a mild, nutty flavor, and melts easily, making it ideal for many uses. Other Italian Fontinas, called fontals, are more widely available and less expensive. Generally mild, Fontina becomes pleasantly nutty as it ages and is an excellent value. Fontina is also made in Denmark, France, and the United States, but these products tend to be blander and firmer than the Italian original.

GOAT CHEESES: This general category includes chèvres, the generic French term for goats' milk cheeses. Among the better known French chèvres are Montrachet, Bûcheron, and banon, which is often sold rolled in savory, sage, or peppercorns or wrapped in chestnut leaves and tied with raffia. Innumerable types and variations of goat cheese are made throughout the world. A burgeoning goat cheese industry exists in the United States; notable American ones include fresh fromage blanc; domed taupière; dry, round crottins; Cheddars; jacks; and cabécou, packed in olive oil and herbs. Fresh mild white goat cheese is creamy, soft, and moist with a sour taste ranging from subtle to strong. Its characteristic graininess increases with age, becoming crumbly rather than spreading smoothly. As the cheese ages, it gets firmer, saltier, and sharper. Gjetost is a Norwegian faintly sweet and caramel-colored cheese made from a combination of goats' and cows' milk whey. Goat cheeses suit the appetizer and dessert tray.

GORGONZOLA: Named for a town outside Milan where this cheese was originally made more than one thousand years ago, Gorgonzola enjoys an acclaimed international reputation. Bluish-green veins streak its ivory interior, lending a sharp contrast to the delicacy of its creamy taste.

GOUDA: The most important Dutch cheese, Gouda accounts for over two-thirds of that country's total production. It has a mild, nutlike flavor close to Edam, but a creamier texture due to its higher butterfat content (about 48 percent compared to Edam's 40 percent). Baby Gouda, weighing no more than a pound, is mild, with a red wax coating; mature Gouda has a yellow coating; and Gouda aged for one year or longer has black wax and a deep golden color.

GRUYÈRE: This sweet, nutty cows' milk cheese hails from a Swiss town of the same name, where it was first made in the twelfth century. It is also produced in other countries, particularly France, and French Comte Gruyère probably dates as far back as the Swiss. The pale yellow interior of this cheese has scattered pea-sized holes. Marketed in one-hundred-pound wheels, Gruyère is prized as a highly flavorful and versatile cheese.

JARLSBERG: A slightly sweet, all-purpose cheese with an elastic texture, Jarlsberg is good both for cooking and for eating as a snack. Widely exported from Norway, it was reinvented there in the 1950s from an old type of cheese. Its lighter version offers an acceptable substitute with considerably less fat.

KASSERI: The original Kasseri comes from Greece and is a sheeps' milk cheese. American Kasseri, made from cows' milk, has a flavor between Cheddar and Parmesan, and a pleasing winey taste. Italian or American Asiago can be a pleasant, slightly salty, and granular substitute.

MASCARPONE: A delectable double or triple cream that has been whipped to a velvety consistency, mascarpone originally was produced in Lombardy. Double-cream cheeses contain 60 percent butterfat or more; triple creams range from 70 to 75 percent butterfat. Excellent American versions of mascarpone are widely available. This creamy cheese is often paired with fresh fruit or flavored with sugar, cinnamon, powdered chocolate, coffee, or liqueurs.

MONTEREY JACK: This mild, semisoft cheese with a somewhat bland flavor was first made by a Scotsman named David Jacks in Monterey, California, in the 1840s. Today it is made from whole, partly skimmed, or skim milk, and some versions are flavored with jalapeño, garlic, or dill. The widely available unripened style is high in moisture, and its good melting properties make it ideal for sandwiches and hot dishes. Aged, it becomes dry Monterey jack, which is butter yellow, firm, and delectably sharp in flavor, ideal for

snacking or grating. The dark brown edible coating is made from oil, cocoa, and black pepper.

MOZZARELLA: Regular (ripened) and fresh mozzarella are both produced in Italy and the United States. In southern Italy, where mozzarella originated, it is still made from pure water and buffalos' milk or part cows' milk and called mozzarella di bufalo. Delicate, soft, and white, it tastes much like a young goat or sheeps' milk cheese. Good quality ripened cows' milk mozzarella is excellent for melting or slicing; sometimes it is rolled in thin slices of prosciutto or pepperoni, or smoked. Inexpensive factory-made mozzarella, marketed in plastic-wrapped balls or oblongs, tends to be firm and somewhat rubbery and stringy when melted; used in lasagne or pizzas, it adds little flavor.

MUENSTER: Irish monks in Alsace, France, first made Muenster in the seventh century. The classic washed-rind version is highly aromatic, spicy, and creamy, ideal with rye bread. Muenster is widely imitated in other countries, although other versions can be bland by comparison with the robust, authentic cheese.

FINLAND

PARMIGIANO REGGIANO: This premier Parmesan has a rich, sharp, complex flavor and granular texture that melts in the mouth. Although Parmesan cheeses are made in Argentina, Australia, and the United States, none compares with Italy's preeminent Parmigiano Reggiano, which hails from the province of Parma and nearby environs. The eighty to eighty-five-pound wheels are marked with a stamp of authenticity and the date of production after they are aged a year. Cheeses aged from eighteen months to two years are called *vecchio*; those labeled *stravecchio* have been aged for three years, while *stravechiones* are four years old. Rarely are they marketed before two years of age. An Italian cheesemaker considers a cheese at its peak of perfection when tiny tears of moisture glisten on the surface after it is split open. Parmigiano is a superb dessert cheese when young; when older it makes an ideal grating cheese.

PECORINO ROMANO: This grayish-white Italian cheese, made from sheeps' milk, comes from central Italy. Often very salty, it has a sharp flavor. Southern Italy produces quantities under the simple name pecorino. This is a classic grating cheese for pasta, pesto, and many other dishes.

PORT-SALUT: This semisoft cheese was first made by Trappist monks in Brittany in the early nineteenth century. Made from cows' milk, the mild, savory flavor and satiny texture of Port-Salut make it an ideal partner for fruit.

PROVOLONE: A southern Italian cows' milk cheese, provolone has a mild, smoky flavor and a golden-brown rind. An excellent cooking cheese, when aged it makes a fine grating cheese.

RICOTTA: This mild, white, slightly grainy fresh cheese has a faintly sweet flavor and is often baked in casseroles. Most Italian ricottas are made from the whey left over from making mozzarella and provolone; American ricottas are usually made from a combination of whey and whole or skim milk.

ROQUEFORT: This premier French blue cheese has been enjoyed since Roman times. Made from sheeps' milk, it is then exposed to a mold known as *Penicillium roqueforti* and aged in the limestone caves of Mount Combalou near the village of Roquefort in southwest France. The trade name is stringently protected; each foil-wrapped cheese carries a label depicting a sheep printed in red ink. Because of its creamy-rich texture and piquant, slightly salty flavor, aficionados prize Roquefort at the end of a meal with a glass of port or a fine Sauternes. It is also popular in salads and spreads.

SAINT-ANDRÉ: This is the most popular and available triple-cream cheese, which means it contains 70 percent or more butterfat. Other popular triple creams include Boursin, available plain or flavored with garlic and herbs or fresh peppercorns; Boursault, which is slightly sour; and Explorateur, which is slightly tart and complex in flavor. All of these cheeses excel with peaches, mangoes, papayas, and kiwifruit.

STILTON: England's king of cheeses derived its name from the village of Stilton, where it was first sold in the eighteenth century. Made from whole cows' milk, it is injected with *Penicillium roqueforti* mold as it ripens. This process creates greenish-blue veins in a very pale yellow interior with a gray, crusty rind. Stilton is an excellent dessert cheese and is often served with port.

Other popular cheeses include Bel Paese, a semisoft Italian cheese, ideal for snacks and dessert or for melting in casseroles or pizza. Havarti, a Danish semisoft cheese with small irregular holes, is mild and tangy when young and sharper when aged. A close cousin to Gruyère, the Swiss cheese raclette is often served melted in a dish by that name. Teleme has a soft, creamy texture similar to Brie and melts beautifully. Samsoe is a Swiss-style Danish cheese with a mild, nutlike flavor. Asiago, a semifirm cheese with a nutty flavor, makes a fine table cheese when young and a grating cheese when aged.

Neufchâtel, which contains 30 percent less fat than standard cream cheese, is also available in a whipped style. Most cream cheese sold in standard-sized rectangles or logs contains vegetable gum; natural cream cheese provides a purer, fine-tasting product. Flavored cream cheeses include Rondele, Alouette, and Danish cream cheese, available in such flavors as garlic, onion, caviar, smoked salmon, peach melba, pineapple, orange, and chocolate.

A CHEESE-TASTING PARTY~ A CHEESE TASTING FOLLOWS THE SAME RATIONALE AS A WINE TASTING. START WITH THE MILDEST CHEESE AND PROGRESS TO THE STRONGEST. FOR AN ALMOST SPUR-OF-THE-MOMENT PARTY THAT REQUIRES NO COOKING, TRY A CHEESE-TASTING BUFFET, MATING EACH CHEESE WITH A COMPLEMENTARY FRUIT OR VEGETABLE. WINE ENHANCES CHEESE AND OFFERS MANY OPTIONS, FROM A TASTING OF CALIFORNIA ZINFANDELS OR FRENCH BEAUJOLAIS, TO A CHOICE OF MERLOTS, PINOT NOIRS, OR CABERNET SAUVIGNONS FROM TWO VINTAGES. OFFER A COMBINATION OF AT LEAST SIX CHEESES, EACH PAIRED WITH A FRUIT OR VEGETABLE:

~ *Jarlsberg with Golden Delicious or Gala apples*

~ *Havarti with red bell peppers*

~ *Gorgonzola with fennel*

~ *Boursin or herb-flavored natural cream cheese with cucumbers*

~ *Port-Salut with Comice pears*

~ *Provolone with pineapple*

~ *Brie with Muscat grapes*

~ *Vermont or Canadian Cheddar with Fuji apples*

~ *Goat cheese with mushrooms*

~ *Baguettes, focaccia, water biscuits*

~ *Wine*

SHOPPING: Count on one-half bottle of wine and 4 ounces of cheese per person. Figure on $1\frac{1}{2}$ whole fruits and a smaller amount of vegetables per person. For 24 guests, offer a combination of 3 cheeses and 3 fruits and 3 cheeses and 3 vegetables. A sample list would include 12 apples, 12 pears, 2 whole pineapples, 8 red peppers, 2 heads fennel, and 4 cucumbers.

SERVING: Let the cheeses warm to room temperature for about 1 hour before serving, depending on the kind of cheese and the heat of the day (see page 10). Serve in wedges or blocks and accompany with a cheese plane, slicer, or cheese knives so guests can cut their own. Arrange and serve the cheeses beginning with the mildest and ending with the strongest in flavor. Thinly slice the baguette, cut the focaccia into squares, and offer the crackers in a basket. If you like, place a different wine at each cheese station.

WINE AND CHEESE COMBINATIONS

With countless varieties of both cheese and wine, the possibilities are endless. Yet certain rules apply. Often, pairing the regional wines with local cheeses makes an ideal combination, such as Muenster with Alsatian Gewürztraminer, chèvres with Sancerre, or Roquefort with Sauternes. Consider other beverages, too: tart cider or Calvados has a natural affinity for soft-ripened cheeses such as Camembert, and beer is a good partner for strong cheeses. Good combinations include:

Asiago with lively Piedmontese reds or Cabernet Sauvignon

Brie or **Camembert** with Cabernet Sauvignon, Bordeaux reds

Cheddar with many reds: Cabernet Sauvignon, Zinfandel, Shiraz, Burgundies; pair the quality of the cheese with a similar-quality wine, or beer

Chèvre: soft types with Merlot, French country reds, and dry whites such as Sauvignon Blanc and Sancerre; aged chèvre, such as taupière or Fourmes, with Cabernet Sauvignon

Emmentaler, **Gruyère**, **Edam**, **Jarlsberg**, and **Gouda** with fruity reds or whites, Pinot Noir

Feta with dry Greek whites, retsina, ouzo

Fontina with Merlot, Pinot Grigio

Gorgonzola with Barbera, Provençal reds

Mascarpone with Moselle, light sweet whites

Monterey jack with Sauvignon Blanc

Mozzarella with a light Chianti

Parmigiano Reggiano with wines of the Piedmont: Barolo, Barbaresco, Chianti, Pinot Noir

Roquefort with late-harvest Zinfandel, minor Sauternes, Rhône reds

Stilton with tawny port, red Rioja, Barolo

ITALY

Chive

Rosemary

fennel

Parsley

Shallots

Mushrooms

North Saskatchewan

Thyme

Bay Leaf

basil

CYPRUS

CRETE O.

APPETIZERS, SOUPS, AND SALADS

CHEESE PROVENÇAL ~ CALIFORNIA GOAT-CHEESE MAKER

LAUREL CHENEL PACKS ROUNDS OF HER CHEESE IN OLIVE OIL AND HERBS.
THE TECHNIQUE WORKS SUPREMELY WELL WITH MONTEREY JACK AND OTHER
CHEESES AS WELL. HERE, HERBS AND RED CHILIES ADD ZEST TO CHEESE FOR A
SWIFT, MAKE-AHEAD APPETIZER THAT TRAVELS EASILY TO A PICNIC OR ALFRESCO
PARTY. THE CRISP VEGETABLES PROVIDE A REFRESHING TEXTURE CONTRAST.

~ 8 ounces Monterey jack, Fontina, Cheddar, Gouda, or Muenster cheese

~ 2 tablespoons mixed minced fresh herbs: thyme, oregano, and rosemary

~ 1 dried hot red chili, halved

~ 1 bay leaf

~ Extra-virgin olive oil (about 1 cup)

~ Sesame crackers or thin baguette slices for serving

~ Fennel stalks, sliced mushrooms, red bell pepper strips, and jícama sticks for serving

Cut the cheese into 1¼-inch cubes and place in a wide-mouthed jar. Sprinkle with the herbs. Add the chili and bay leaf. Pour in oil to just cover the cheese. Cover and refrigerate for 3 or 4 days, or longer. Accompany with crackers or baguette slices. Serve the cheese from the jar and accompany with a tray of vegetables.

MAKES 6 TO 8 SERVINGS

GORGONZOLA HERB DIP WITH VEGETABLES~

THIS LIGHT CHEESE DIP FOR RAW AND COOKED VEGETABLES ALSO DOES WONDERS FOR A BAKED POTATO AND ENHANCES A PLATE OF SLICED TOMATOES OR CHILLED BROCCOLI. FOR A FIRST COURSE, SPOON IT INTO SMALL STONEWARE DISHES OR SOUFFLÉ MOLDS TO ACCOMPANY A PLATE OF RAW MUSHROOMS, FENNEL SLICES, AND RED AND GOLD CHERRY TOMATOES.

In a blender or food processor, process the shallot, parsley, chives, thyme or tarragon, cottage cheese, yogurt, and vinegar until smooth. Add the Gorgonzola and process for a few seconds to blend it in. Turn into a serving container and chill. Serve with a basket or platter of raw vegetables or hot baked potatoes.

MAKES ABOUT 2 CUPS

~ *1 shallot, minced*

~ *2 tablespoons minced fresh flat-leaf (Italian) parsley*

~ *2 tablespoons minced fresh chives*

~ *2 teaspoons minced fresh thyme or tarragon, or ½ teaspoon dried thyme or tarragon*

~ *1 cup (8 ounces) cottage cheese*

~ *½ cup plain yogurt*

~ *1 tablespoon balsamic vinegar*

~ *2 to 3 ounces Gorgonzola or other creamy blue cheese*

~ *Raw vegetables or baked potatoes for serving*

A DOZEN CHEESE PARTY SNACKS

These cheese nibbles make easy-to-pass finger food for cocktails or teatime.

Brush baguette slices with garlic oil, toast until golden, and spread with goat cheese or sliced mozzarella. Top with drained oil-packed sun-dried tomatoes and basil sprigs.

On wooden skewers, alternate cubes of Jarlsberg, Cheddar, or jack cheese, and strawberries, melon balls, and fresh pineapple cubes. Or alternate seedless red and green grapes with cubes of jack or white Cheddar. Or pair cubes of papaya and dry jack cheese on skewers.

Top slices of kiwifruit with Explorateur or a fruit-flavored natural cream cheese for a tea snack. Serve on unsalted crackers or split biscuits.

Spread dark-rye bread squares with whipped natural cream cheese and top with cooked small shrimp and watercress sprigs.

Top sliced cucumber rounds with cream cheese flavored with smoked salmon or caviar, and dill sprigs.

Stuff fennel stalks or celery sticks with Gorgonzola or another blue cheese and sprinkle with toasted walnuts.

Wrap a lemon leaf or a preserved grape leaf around a wedge of Fontina or jack, skewer with a toothpick, and grill until the cheese is warm.

Stuff cherry tomato halves with herb-flavored fresh mild white goat cheese or natural cream cheese and tuck in a basil leaf.

Place a dollop of fresh mild white goat cheese or mango chutney–flavored natural cream cheese on red or green endive leaves and top each one with 2 cooked small bay shrimp.

Dollop dried apricots with Saint-André and sprinkle with chopped toasted pistachios or chopped peeled toasted hazelnuts.

Halve figs and spread with mascarpone and a strip of prosciutto. Or top with Gorgonzola and broil until heated through.

Peel, halve, pit, and quarter peaches. Dollop with Saint-André and sprinkle with toasted pine nuts.

Spread toasted baguette slices with fresh mild white goat cheese and top with a red pepper pesto, an olive pesto, or a few dried cherries.

GOUGÈRE CHEESE PUFFS ~ GOLDEN SPHERES FLECKED WITH MELTING CHEESE PROVIDE A SAVORY APPETIZER OR A HOT BREAD FOR A SUNDAY BRUNCH. IN THE FRENCH MODE, YOU MIGHT SERVE THESE WITH KIRS: APÉRITIFS OF WHITE WINE WITH A SPLASH OF CRÈME DE CASSIS.

Preheat the oven to 375°F. In a medium saucepan, heat the butter, milk, salt, and mustard and bring to a rolling boil. Add the flour all at once and beat constantly with a wooden spoon over medium heat until the mixture leaves the sides of the pan and forms a ball. Remove from heat and beat in the eggs one at a time, beating until smooth. Mix in the cheese. Drop tablespoonfuls 2 inches apart on a buttered baking sheet. Sprinkle with the nuts. Bake for 25 to 30 minutes, or until golden brown. Serve hot or reheat.

MAKES ABOUT 2 DOZEN PUFFS

~ 5 tablespoons butter

~ 1 cup milk

~ 1/4 teaspoon each salt and dry mustard

~ 1 cup unbleached all-purpose flour

~ 4 eggs

~ 1 cup (4 ounces) shredded Gruyère, Jarlsberg, or Samsoe cheese

~ 1/4 cup chopped almonds or peeled toasted hazelnuts

BAKED BRIE DRESSED FOR A PARTY

WARM BRIE WITH A PECAN CAP~ WITH A TOASTY NUT CROWN AND A WREATH OF RED AND GREEN SLICED APPLES, WARM BRIE MAKES A COLORFUL, YEAR-AROUND APPETIZER. SLICED PEARS AND RED AND GREEN SEEDLESS GRAPES ARE OTHER APPEALING FRUITS TO SERVE.

~ *One 1-pound wheel of Brie cheese*

~ *2 tablespoons butter, melted*

~ *1/2 cup (2 ounces) pecans or sliced almonds*

~ *4 sliced apples, preferably both red and green*

~ *Wafer crackers or toasted baguette slices for serving*

Preheat the oven to 350°F. Place the Brie on an oven-proof serving dish. Brush the top with butter and toss the nuts in the remaining butter. Scatter the nuts over the top of the cheese. Bake in the oven for 8 to 10 minutes, or until the cheese softens and the nuts are lightly toasted. Serve surrounded with sliced apples and pass a basket of crackers or toasted baguette slices.

MAKES 8 TO 10 SERVINGS

APRICOT AND PINE NUT–CROWNED BRIE ~ ORANGE LIQUEUR–SCENTED APRICOTS AND CRISP NUT MEATS CLOAKING WARM BRIE MAKE A SUBLIME SPREAD FOR FRENCH BREAD. SERVE THIS AS A DELECTABLE COMBINATION CHEESE AND DESSERT COURSE.

27

Preheat the oven to 350°F. With a sharp paring knife, cut off and remove the top rind of the Brie. Place the cheese on an ovenproof serving dish. Prick the top with a fork in a dozen places and drizzle with ½ tablespoon of the liqueur or brandy. Toss the remaining 1½ tablespoons liqueur or brandy with the apricots, raisins, and pine nuts, and scatter this mixture over the top of the cheese. Bake in the oven for 8 to 10 minutes, or until the cheese softens. Serve with crackers or sliced bread.

MAKES 8 TO 10 SERVINGS

~ *One 1-pound wheel of Brie cheese*

~ *2 tablespoons orange Curaçao, Cointreau, Cognac, or brandy*

~ *⅓ cup dried apricots, cut into ¼-inch strips*

~ *3 tablespoons golden raisins*

~ *3 tablespoons pine nuts*

~ *Wafer crackers on toasted baguette slices for serving*

QUESADILLAS WITH MANGO AND CHILIES ~

THIS EXOTIC HOT SNACK MAKES A TASTE-TINGLING APPETIZER OR A NOVEL ACCOMPANIMENT TO A SOUP OR SALAD LUNCHEON. I LIKE TO PARTNER THE WARM TORTILLA TRIANGLES WITH A BLACK BEAN SOUP OR A MEXICAN SALAD OF SLICED JÍCAMA, ORANGES, AND CUCUMBERS.

~ Six 8-inch flour tortillas

~ 2 cups (8 ounces) shredded Monterey jack cheese

~ 1 can (4 ounces) diced green chilies

~ 1 mango or small papaya, peeled, thinly sliced, and cut into 1-inch pieces

Preheat the oven to 250°F. Lay out 3 of the tortillas. Sprinkle with half of the cheese and scatter the chilies and sliced mango or papaya over. Cover with the remaining cheese and top with the remaining tortillas. Heat a large skillet over medium heat and cook the tortillas, one at a time, carefully turning each one to brown both sides, until the cheese is melted. Place on an ovenproof dish and keep warm in the oven until all are cooked. Transfer to a board, cut into wedges, and serve at once.

MAKES 18 APPETIZERS

VARIATION: Instead of the mango or papaya, you may substitute sliced peaches or nectarines. Or, for another cheese filling, spread the tortillas with 6 ounces of room-temperature goat cheese and top with 1 cup snipped drained oil-cured sun-dried tomatoes.

SADIE'S CHEESE STRAWS ~ THESE CRISPY CHEESE WAFERS FROM A FRIEND'S SOUTHERN COOK MAKE DELECTABLE BITEFULS TO PASS WITH WINE OR COCKTAILS. OR MATE THEM WITH A FRUIT OR SEAFOOD SALAD LUNCHEON. THE DOUGH IS EASY TO HANDLE WITHOUT CHILLING.

~ 1¼ cups unbleached all-purpose flour

~ 1 teaspoon salt

~ 2 teaspoons dry mustard

~ ¼ teaspoon ground ginger

~ Dash of cayenne pepper

~ ½ cup (1 stick) cold unsalted butter

~ 1 cup (4 ounces) shredded sharp Cheddar cheese

~ 5 to 6 tablespoons ice cold water

Preheat the oven to 425°F. Stir together the flour, salt, mustard, ginger, and cayenne. Using a pastry blender or 2 knives, cut in the butter and cheese until the mixture resembles fine crumbs. Sprinkle the water over the flour mixture, 1 tablespoon at a time, and pat together into a ball.

Roll the dough out ¼ inch thick on a lightly floured board. Cut the dough into strips ⅜ inch wide and 4 inches long. Place on an ungreased baking sheet and bake in the oven for 8 minutes, or until golden brown. Serve warm or let cool on a rack. Store in an airtight container.

MAKES ABOUT 7 DOZEN CHEESE STRAWS

CHEESE PITAS ~ THESE TRIANGULAR GREEK APPETIZER PASTRIES CONSIST OF A CRISP WRAPPER OF THE TISSUE-THIN DOUGH CALLED FILO, OR PHYLLO, WITH AN HERB-FLAVORED CHEESE FILLING. ASSEMBLE THE PITAS IN ADVANCE AND FREEZE THEM, IF DESIRED, THEN BAKE THEM JUST BEFORE GUESTS ARRIVE. CHEESE PITAS MAKE A SPLENDID PRELUDE TO A MEDITERRANEAN REPAST OF GRILLED SWORDFISH OR LAMB KABOBS, PILAF, ZUCCHINI STREWN WITH FRESH OREGANO, AND MUSCAT GRAPES OR NECTARINES.

Preheat the oven to 375°F. Place the 4 cheeses, parsley, and chives in a mixing bowl or a food processor and mix until blended. Mix in the egg, egg yolk, and nutmeg. Lay out one sheet of filo and cut it into 3-inch-wide strips about 12 inches long. (Keep the remaining filo covered with plastic wrap to prevent it from drying out.) Brush each strip lightly with melted butter. Place 1 rounded teaspoon of the cheese mixture on one corner of the strip; fold the corner over to make a triangle. Continue folding the filo over in triangles, like folding a flag. Repeat until all of the filo is filled. (If desired, freeze at this point. Let thaw before baking.) Place seam-side down on a baking sheet. Bake in the oven for 15 minutes, or until golden brown. Serve hot.

MAKES ABOUT 5 DOZEN APPETIZERS

~ 8 ounces each *feta cheese and ricotta*

~ *1/2 cup (2 ounces) grated pecorino romano or Parmigiano Reggiano cheese*

~ *3/4 cup (3 ounces) grated Gruyère or Samsoe cheese*

~ 2 tablespoons each *minced fresh flat-leaf (Italian) parsley and fresh chives*

~ *1 egg*

~ *1 egg yolk*

~ *1/8 teaspoon ground nutmeg*

~ *8 ounces (about 10 sheets) filo dough*

~ *6 tablespoons unsalted butter, melted*

EIGHT FRUIT, CHEESE, AND NUT SALADS

Choose a light vinaigrette to dress these piquant first-course salads. For a good combination, blend ¼ cup fruity olive oil, 1½ tablespoons raspberry vinegar, 1 teaspoon cassis syrup, 1 minced shallot, 2 teaspoons Dijon mustard, and salt and freshly ground pepper to taste.

PEAR, GORGONZOLA, AND WALNUT SALAD: Arrange a fan of Belgian endive leaves on salad plates and top with sliced Comice pears, crumbled Gorgonzola, Cambozola, or other blue cheese, and a few toasted walnuts. Drizzle with vinaigrette.

PAPAYA, GOAT CHEESE, AND PISTACHIO SALAD: Arrange baby greens or arugula and butter lettuce on salad plates. Top with sliced papaya and nuggets of fresh mild white goat cheese, and scatter toasted pistachios over. Drizzle with vinaigrette.

BLUEBERRY, BRIE, AND PECAN SALAD: Toss red oakleaf and butter lettuce with vinaigrette and arrange on salad plates. Scatter with blueberries, diced Brie, and toasted pecans.

NECTARINE, SAINT-ANDRÉ, AND PINE NUT SALAD: Toss mixed greens with vinaigrette and arrange on salad plates. Top with a pinwheel of sliced nectarines, nuggets of Saint-André or Explorateur cheese, and toasted pine nuts.

SPINACH SALAD WITH TANGERINES, PINE NUTS, AND PARMIGIANO REGGIANO: Toss spinach leaves with vinaigrette and arrange on salad plates. Top with tangerine sections, avocado chunks, shavings of Parmigiano Reggiano cheese, and toasted pine nuts.

GRAPES, GORGONZOLA, AND ALMOND SALAD: Toss mixed greens with vinaigrette and sprinkle with red seedless grapes, nuggets of Gorgonzola, and toasted slivered almonds.

APPLE, JARLSBERG, AND HAZELNUT SALAD: Toss mixed greens with vinaigrette and diced Fuji or Jonathan apples, finely diced Jarlsberg cheese, and chopped peeled toasted hazelnuts.

STRAWBERRY, SPINACH, AND FETA SALAD: Toss spinach leaves and a few strawberries with vinaigrette and sprinkle with crumbled feta and toasted pistachios.

MARITATA SOUP ~ THIS CREAMY-RICH ITALIAN WEDDING SOUP IS AN ELEGANT PASS-AROUND STARTER FOR A DINNER FEATURING GRILLED SAGE-STUFFED CHICKEN, ROASTED NEW POTATOES AND MUSHROOMS, AND FRESH RASPBERRIES WITH FRAMBOISE OVER VANILLA-BEAN ICE CREAM.

In a small bowl, beat together the butter, cheeses, and egg yolks; mix in the cream. In a large saucepan, heat the chicken broth and wine to steaming; pour a little broth into the cheese mixture, then stir it into the remaining broth in the pan. Heat through, but do not boil, stirring until blended. Season with salt and pepper. Ladle into small cups for sipping or into bowls for table service. Sprinkle with chives or parsley.

MAKES 6 SERVINGS

~ 2 tablespoons unsalted butter at room temperature

~ $1/2$ cup (2 ounces) grated fontina, Samsoe, or Monterey jack cheese

~ $1/4$ cup grated pecorino romano or Parmesan cheese

~ 2 egg yolks

~ $1/2$ cup heavy (whipping) cream

~ 3 cups homemade or canned low-salt chicken broth

~ $1/2$ cup dry white wine

~ Salt and white pepper to taste

~ Chopped fresh chives or minced fresh flat-leaf (Italian) parsley for garnish

COBB SALAD ~ TWO CHEESES STRIPE THIS POPULAR, DECADES-OLD SALAD CREATED AT THE FAMED HOLLYWOOD BROWN DERBY RESTAURANT BY OWNER BOB COBB. PROSCIUTTO IS A NICE STAND-IN FOR THE TRADITIONAL BACON.

~ 1 small head romaine, chopped

~ 1 bunch watercress, stemmed

~ 2 hard-cooked eggs

~ 1 large tomato, chopped

~ 2 cooked chicken breast halves, cut into strips, or 1 1/2 cups cooked turkey, diced

~ 1 cup (4 ounces) Gruyère, Jarlsberg, or Emmentaler cheese, diced

~ 1 ripe avocado, peeled, pitted, and diced

~ 2 ounces thinly sliced prosciutto, cut into strips, or 4 slices crisp-cooked bacon, crumbled

~ 1/2 cup (2 ounces) Gorgonzola, Roquefort, or blue cheese, crumbled

~ 1/4 cup minced fresh flat-leaf (Italian) parsley

~ Vinaigrette (recipe follows)

In a large salad bowl, toss the romaine and watercress. Chop the whites and yolks of the eggs separately. Place the tomato and chicken or turkey over the center of the greens. Arrange the diced cheese, avocado, and egg whites on one side of the center and the prosciutto, egg yolks, and crumbled cheese on the other side. Sprinkle with the parsley. Toss with the vinaigrette at the table.

MAKES 4 SERVINGS

VINAIGRETTE DRESSING: Mix together 3 tablespoons each olive oil and canola oil, 2 tablespoons red or white wine vinegar, salt and freshly ground black pepper to taste, 1 teaspoon Dijon mustard, and 1 minced shallot.

CHILE CON QUESO ~ THIS EASY-TO-ASSEMBLE HOT MEXICAN APPETIZER IS IDEAL FOR AN INFORMAL GATHERING OR A GARDEN PARTY. ALLOW THE CHEESES TO WARM TO ROOM TEMPERATURE BEFORE USING.

37

In a stove-to-table skillet over medium heat, heat the oil and sauté the onion, garlic, and cumin until soft, about 5 to 7 minutes. Stir in the tomatoes and chili or pepper and sauté until the vegetables are soft, about 3 to 5 minutes. Sprinkle in the cheeses and cook over low heat, stirring, just until melted; do not boil. Keep warm over a warmer or a hot tray. Accompany with baskets of chips and vegetables.

MAKES ABOUT 4 ENTREE SERVINGS OR 12 APPETIZER SERVINGS

VARIATION: Substitute 8 ounces fresh mild white goat cheese for the Teleme, Monterey jack, or Cheddar cheese.

~ *1 tablespoon olive oil*

~ *1 onion, finely chopped*

~ *1 large garlic clove, chopped*

~ *1/4 teaspoon ground cumin*

~ *2 Roma tomatoes, chopped*

~ *1 fresh Anaheim chili or 1/2 red or green bell pepper, cored, seeded, and finely chopped*

~ *2 cups (8 ounces) sliced Teleme cheese or shredded Monterey jack or Cheddar cheese at room temperature*

~ *4 ounces natural cream cheese, broken into small chunks, at room temperature*

~ *Blue or yellow corn tortilla chips for serving*

~ *Jícama strips, red bell pepper strips, diagonally sliced zucchini chips for serving*

FRENCH ONION SOUP WITH CHEESE

CROÛTONS ~ YEARS AGO THE BUSTLING LES HALLES PARISIAN FOOD

MARKET POPULARIZED THIS CHEESE-GRATINÉED SOUP. THERE A COLORFUL

MINGLING OF SOCIETY FOLK AND WORKERS DOWNED BOWLFULS IN THE PRE-DAWN

HOURS. THOUGH THE MARKET MOVED AWAY, THE SOUP LIVES ON.

~ *4 large yellow onions, sliced*

~ *1 tablespoon olive oil*

~ *4 cups homemade or canned low-salt beef broth*

~ *$^1/_2$ cup dry red wine such as Merlot, Zinfandel, or Pinot Noir*

~ *Freshly ground black pepper to taste*

~ *Four $^1/_2$ inch-thick slices French bread, toasted and buttered*

~ *$^1/_3$ cup each shredded Parmesan and Gruyère cheese, mixed*

In a large soup kettle over low heat, slowly cook the onions in the oil until golden brown, about 10 minutes, stirring occasionally. Add the broth, wine, and pepper, and simmer for 30 minutes. Ladle into heavy ovenproof soup bowls. Float a slice of toasted bread on each bowlful and sprinkle with the mixed cheeses. Place under the broiler until the cheese melts and lightly browns, about 2 minutes.

MAKES 4 SERVINGS

SANDWICHES, PASTAS, AND PIZZAS

Fig. 115.

BRUSCHETTA WITH TOMATOES AND ASIAGO~

IN THE MEDITERRANEAN REGION, CLASSIC TOMATO- AND BASIL-TOPPED BRUSCHETTA IS A POPULAR NOONTIME MEAL WITH NUGGETS OF CHEESE ALONGSIDE OR WAFER-THIN SHAVINGS ON TOP. IN THE EVENING, IT IS A CUSTOMARY APPETIZER IN ALFRESCO TRATTORIAS AND TAVERNAS. ON A HILLTOP IN CRETE BESIDE THE VINEYARDS OF THE BOUTARI WINERY, THIS WAS THE FIRST COURSE FOR A LUNCH OF GARLICKY ROAST POTATOES AND LAMB, WITH CANDIED FIGS FOR DESSERT.

~ *4 thick slices country bread*

~ *2 garlic cloves, peeled and cut in half*

~ *Extra-virgin olive oil*

~ *8 large basil leaves, minced*

~ *2 vine-ripened Roma tomatoes, peeled, seeded, and chopped*

~ *Salt and freshly ground black pepper to taste*

~ *12 Kalamata or other black olives*

~ *1 cup (4 ounces) diced Asiago or Kasseri cheese*

Grill or lightly toast the bread. Rub one side with the garlic and drizzle with olive oil. Stir the basil and a spoonful of oil into the tomatoes; season with salt and pepper. Arrange the toast on plates, spoon the tomatoes over, and ring with olives and cheese.

MAKES 4 SERVINGS

VARIATIONS:

BRUSCHETTA WITH RED ONIONS AND FETA~ Instead of the tomato topping, finely chop 1 large red onion and sauté in 2 tablespoons olive oil. Season with 2 teaspoons minced fresh oregano and salt and pepper to taste. Spoon over the garlic toast and scatter 2 ounces crumbled feta over. Accompany with a dozen small ripe Mediterranean olives.

BRUSCHETTA WITH MUSHROOMS AND GOAT CHEESE~ Instead of the tomato topping, slice 8 ounces white button mushrooms and toss in 2 tablespoons olive oil, 1 tablespoon fresh lemon juice, 1 teaspoon minced fresh thyme, 1 tablespoon minced fresh flat-leaf (Italian) parsley, and salt and freshly ground black pepper to taste. Spoon over the garlic toast and dollop with 2 ounces aged or fresh mild white goat cheese such as banon or pyramide.

BRUSCHETTA WITH RICOTTA AND NECTARINES OR FIGS~ Omit the garlic on the toast and spread the toast with 1/2 cup whole-milk ricotta, drizzle with 2 tablespoons cassis syrup, and top with slices of 2 nectarines or 4 figs. Serve as dessert or an afternoon snack.

A DOZEN SPLIT-SECOND SANDWICHES

GRUYÈRE, BLACK FOREST HAM, AND RED ONION OPEN-FACED SANDWICHES: Top crusty country bread with sliced Gruyère, Black Forest ham, tapenade, thinly sliced red onions, spinach, and sliced tomato. Serve open-faced.

JARLSBERG, CHICKEN, AND SUN-DRIED TOMATO ON SOURDOUGH: Fill buttered sourdough French bread slices with sliced Jarlsberg, sliced roasted chicken breast, and drained oil-packed sun-dried tomatoes. Serve with cornichons.

CROQUE MONSIEUR: Spread 2 slices firm white bread with butter and Dijon mustard and fill with thinly sliced Emmentaler and sliced ham. Butter the outside of the sandwich. Cook in a skillet, turning to brown both sides and pressing down with a metal spatula to compact the sandwich. Or, cook in a sandwich toaster until golden brown.

MONTEREY JACK, CHUTNEY, AND PROSCIUTTO SANDWICH: Fill buttered crusty bread with sliced Monterey jack, mango chutney, and sliced prosciutto.

PASTRAMI AND MUENSTER ON RYE: Spread dark Russian rye with butter and Dijon mustard and fill with thinly sliced pastrami, sliced Muenster, a few dried cherries, and butter lettuce. Replace the lettuce with a spoonful of well-drained sauerkraut to make a Reuben sandwich.

HAVARTI, SPROUTS, AND RED PEPPERS ON RYE: Spread light rye bread with butter and Dijon mustard, and fill with sliced Havarti cheese, alfalfa sprouts, and strips of red bell pepper.

GOAT CHEESE AND SMOKED SALMON BAGELS: Split a plain or onion bagel and spread one half with room-temperature mild white goat cheese or natural cream cheese. Layer with thinly sliced smoked salmon, slivered red onion, if desired, and watercress.

GREEK COUNTRY-STYLE PITA: Cut a white or whole-wheat pita bread in half and fill each half with a Greek country-style salad of diced cucumber, diced tomato, and crumbled feta cheese drizzled with olive oil and seasoned with minced fresh oregano and freshly ground pepper. Accompany with Kalamata or other black olives.

GRILLED EGGPLANT AND MOZZARELLA BAGUETTE: Grill or roast eggplant slices and layer on a split baguette along with sliced mozzarella, sliced tomatoes or roasted red bell peppers, and fresh basil leaves.

RICOTTA AND SUN-DRIED TOMATO BAGUETTE: Spread a split baguette with ricotta or room-temperature natural cream cheese, drained oil-packed sun-dried tomato halves, and arugula leaves.

FOCACCIA WITH FONTINA, PROSCIUTTO, AND RED ONIONS: Warm the focaccia in the oven, split it, and fill it with sliced Fontina, thinly sliced prosciutto, a few slices of sweet red onions, and fresh basil leaves.

CRAB, AVOCADO, AND JARLSBERG MUFFIN: Butter and lightly toast split English muffins. Spread with mayonnaise, sprinkle with fresh crabmeat or small shrimp, and top with sliced Jarlsberg or Monterey jack cheese. Place under the broiler until the cheese melts. Top each half with avocado slices and a cherry tomato half.

FOCACCIA WITH GORGONZOLA ~ CRUSTY OUTSIDE AND

SPRINGY WITHIN, FOCACCIA IS A BELOVED ITALIAN FLAT BREAD WITH A HOMESPUN

GOODNESS. ITS DIMPLED SURFACE CAN TAKE ON MANY FLAVOR VARIATIONS, AND

GORGONZOLA GIVES IT CACHET.

~ *¹⁄₄ cup warm (105° to 115°F) water*

~ *1 package active dry yeast*

~ *1¹⁄₄ cups water at room temperature*

~ *2 tablespoons sugar or honey*

~ *1¹⁄₂ tablespoons olive oil*

~ *3 cups unbleached all-purpose flour*

~ *1 tablespoon each minced fresh sage and rosemary, or ³⁄₄ teaspoon each dried herbs*

~ *1¹⁄₂ teaspoons salt*

~ *1 cup (4 ounces) Gorgonzola or other creamy blue cheese, crumbled*

~ *Olive oil for brushing*

Place the warm water in a large mixing bowl and stir in the yeast; let stand until dissolved and puffy, about 10 minutes. Stir in the room-temperature water, the sugar or honey, and oil. Whisk in 1 cup of the flour, the herbs, and salt. Mix in the remaining flour, ¹⁄₂ cup at a time. Knead on a lightly floured surface until smooth and satiny, about 2 to 3 minutes. Place the dough in an oiled bowl, cover, and let rise in a warm place until doubled, about 1¹⁄₂ hours.

Punch the dough down, turn it out on a lightly floured board, and knead a few times. Roll out the dough to fit a 10-by-15-inch baking pan. Place the dough in the greased pan and dimple the dough with your fingers by making depressions about 1 inch apart. Brush the dough with olive oil. Place the crumbled cheese in the depressions. Cover with a towel and let rise until doubled.

Preheat the oven to 425°F. Bake the focaccia on the middle rack of the oven for 20 minutes, or until golden brown. Slice and serve warm, or serve at room temperature.

MAKES I LARGE RECTANGULAR OR TWO 9-INCH ROUND LOAVES

VARIATIONS:

FOCACCIA WITH MOZZARELLA AND RED ONIONS~ Brush the dimpled dough with olive oil and stud the dough with ¾ cup (3 ounces) diced fresh mozzarella or Monterey jack cheese and 2 sweet red or white onions that have been chopped and sautéed in 2 tablespoons olive oil until soft. Sprinkle with ¼ cup pine nuts. Let rise before baking.

FOCACCIA WITH RED GRAPES AND KASSERI~ Brush the dimpled dough with olive oil. Instead of Gorgonzola, stud the dough with 2 cups seedless red grapes. Sprinkle with 2 tablespoons minced fresh rosemary and fresh sage leaves. Sprinkle lightly with coarse salt and sugar. Let rise and bake. While the bread is still warm, scatter ¾ cup (3 ounces) slivered Kasseri or Asiago cheese over it.

FOCACCIA WITH SAGE AND PECORINO ROMANO~ Brush the dimpled dough with olive oil and cover the surface with fresh sage leaves and shavings of 2 or 3 ounces pecorino romano cheese. Let rise before baking.

Neufchâtel

chive dill basil

SMOKED SALMON LAVOSH ROLL ~ LAVOSH, AN

ARMENIAN-STYLE LARGE ROUND CRACKER, FORMS A BASE FOR THIS PINWHEEL

APPETIZER, WHICH IS EASILY VARIED WITH OTHER FILLINGS. THE ONLY

TRICK TO ITS PREPARATION IS SOAKING THE LAVOSH ENOUGH SO THAT IT ROLLS

WITHOUT CRACKING.

Dampen one large or two smaller kitchen towels and wring out the excess moisture. Moisten the lavosh well on both sides under cold running water. Place darker-side down between 2 layers of damp towel and refrigerate until soft and pliable, about 1 hour. Place on a work surface. Mix the cheese and mustard and spread over the bread. Cover with salmon, chicken, or turkey. Top with tomatoes, basil, and romaine, stopping about 3 inches from the far edge. Sprinkle with dill or chives. Lift the towel to gently but firmly roll the bread up jelly-roll fashion. Wrap in plastic wrap and chill for 1 to 24 hours. Serve cut into crosswise ¾-inch-thick slices.

MAKES 16 APPETIZERS

~ 1 large round lavosh cracker bread

~ 1 cup (4 ounces) natural or whipped Neufchâtel cream cheese at room temperature

~ 2 teaspoons Dijon mustard

~ 4 ounces thinly sliced smoked or flaked baked salmon or thinly sliced smoked chicken or turkey breast

~ 2 large tomatoes, sliced as thin as possible

~ ½ cup fresh basil leaves

~ 4 or 5 outer leaves of romaine lettuce, center ribs removed

~ Minced fresh dill or chives to taste

CRISP ROMAN PIZZAS ~

DOUGH

~ 1 cup warm (105° to 115°F) water

~ 1 envelope active dry yeast

~ 1 teaspoon sugar or honey

~ 1 cup plus 2 tablespoons unbleached all-purpose flour

~ 3/4 teaspoon salt

~ 1 tablespoon olive oil

~ 3/4 cup whole-wheat flour

~ 1/4 cup wheat bran

To make the dough: Place the water in a large bowl and stir in the yeast and sugar or honey. Let stand until dissolved and puffy, about 10 minutes. Mix in the unbleached flour, salt, and oil. Gradually add the whole-wheat flour and bran, and mix until the dough cleans the side of the bowl. Turn out on a lightly floured board and knead a few times until the dough is no longer sticky. Place in an oiled bowl, cover with a towel, and let rise in a warm place until doubled, about 45 minutes. Gently remove the dough from the bowl and cut into 4 equal sections. Use immediately, or wrap each piece loosely in plastic wrap and refrigerate for up to 2 days.

At least 20 minutes before baking, preheat the oven to 475°F with a baking stone inside, if you have one. Cut one piece of dough in half, roll each piece into a 6-by-10-inch oval, and place on a greased baking pan, or on an oiled sheet of aluminum foil to slip directly onto the hot baking stone.

Meanwhile, to make the filling: In a medium skillet, heat the oil over medium heat and sauté the onion for 5 minutes or until soft, then push to the sides of the pan and sauté the zucchini for 2 minutes. Spread the dough with the pizza or marinara sauce and spoon the vegetables over. Scatter the tomatoes over and sprinkle with the cheese and nuts. Bake it for 6 minutes, or until the crust is crisp and browned. Sprinkle with the herbs.

MAKES TWO 10-INCH OVAL PIZZAS, WITH ENOUGH DOUGH FOR 6 MORE 10-INCH PIZZAS

VARIATION: In a medium skillet, heat 1 tablespoon oil and sauté 2 minced shallots until soft, about 5 minutes. Add 4 ounces mushrooms and sauté until glazed, about 2 minutes. Spoon over the dough and top with 1 ounce julienned prosciutto or ham and 2 ounces thinly sliced Gruyère or Jarlsberg cheese. Bake as directed. Remove from the oven and sprinkle with herbs.

FILLING

~ 1 tablespoon olive oil

~ 1 small red or yellow onion, chopped

~ 2 zucchini, thinly sliced

~ $1/3$ cup pizza sauce or marinara sauce

~ 12 drained oil-cured sun-dried tomatoes

~ 2 ounces mozzarella or Monterey jack cheese, thinly sliced

~ 2 tablespoons pine nuts

~ Fresh basil or oregano leaves

ORZO WITH FETA AND SUN-DRIED

TOMATOES ~ BARLEY-SHAPED PASTA MAKES A FINE COLD SALAD TO

CARRY ON A PICNIC OR TO BRING TO A POTLUCK. AUGMENT THE ALFRESCO MEAL

WITH ROAST CHICKEN AND COLD ASPARAGUS SPEARS.

~ 1 cup (6 ounces) orzo

~ ¼ cup olive oil

~ 3 tablespoons fresh lemon juice

~ 2 teaspoons stone-ground mustard

~ 1 shallot or green onion, minced

~ 1 teaspoon dried dill

~ 2 teaspoons fresh oregano, or ½ teaspoon dried oregano

~ Salt and freshly ground pepper to taste

~ ¼ cup minced fresh flat-leaf (Italian) parsley

~ ½ cup drained oil-packed sun-dried tomatoes, snipped

~ ¾ cup (3 ounces) crumbled feta cheese

~ ⅓ cup toasted pine nuts or coarsely chopped toasted pistachios

~ Arugula or oak leaf lettuce leaves

In a large pot of boiling salted water, cook the orzo until al dente, about 12 to 15 minutes; drain and let cool for a few minutes. In a medium bowl, stir together the oil, lemon juice, mustard, shallot or green onion, dill, oregano, and salt and pepper. Add the pasta and toss to coat. Stir in the parsley, tomatoes, and feta. Chill. When ready to serve, sprinkle with the nuts and tuck arugula or lettuce around the edge of the bowl.

MAKES 4 TO 6 SERVINGS

By day

Musta...

parsley

oregano

dill

English Channel

BAY
OF
BISCAY

FRAN...

Bordeaux

feta
cheese

a
fine
cold
salad to
carry on
a
picnic

WHOLE-WHEAT SPAGHETTI WITH LEEKS AND BRIE ~

WHOLE-WHEAT PASTA LENDS A TASTY DIMENSION TO THIS FAST, LAST-MINUTE DISH. WHEN TOSSED, THE HOT PASTA GENTLY COOKS THE LEEK SAUCE AND MELTS THE CHEESE. A SPINACH SALAD, CRUSTY COUNTRY BREAD, AND STRAWBERRIES WITH RASPBERRY AND VANILLA FROZEN YOGURT ARE IDEAL COMPANIONS.

~ *1 dried red chili pepper, crushed*

~ *6 ounces dried whole-wheat spaghetti*

~ *2 leeks (white part only), chopped*

~ *2 tablespoons olive oil*

~ *2 egg yolks*

~ *$1/4$ cup heavy (whipping) cream*

~ *2 ounces Brie, fresh mild white goat cheese, mascarpone, or shredded mozzarella cheese at room temperature*

~ *$1/4$ cup grated pecorino romano or Parmigiano Reggiano cheese, plus extra for the table*

~ *$1/4$ cup minced fresh flat-leaf (Italian) parsley*

~ *Salt and freshly ground black pepper to taste*

Add the crushed pepper to a large pot of salted boiling water. Add the spaghetti and cook just until al dente, about 10 to 12 minutes. Meanwhile, in a medium skillet, sauté the leeks in oil over medium low heat until soft, about 8 minutes. In a shallow serving bowl, beat the egg yolks and mix in the cream, two cheeses, parsley, salt and pepper, and leeks. Add about $1/3$ cup of the pasta cooking water to the leek sauce. Drain the spaghetti and toss with the sauce. Serve with extra grated cheese at the table.

MAKES 2 TO 3 ENTREE SERVINGS

FETTUCCINE WITH MUSHROOMS, GOAT CHEESE, AND PINE NUTS ~ TANGY GOAT CHEESE AND SWEET PINE NUTS MINGLE WITH WOODSY MUSHROOMS TO MAKE A FAST SAUCE FOR FETTUCCINE. SERVE WITH A SALAD OF PEARS, ENDIVE, AND TOASTED HAZELNUTS.

In a large pot of boiling salted water, cook the pasta until just al dente, about 3 to 4 minutes for fresh pasta and 8 to 10 minutes for dried.

Meanwhile, in a medium skillet over medium-low heat, sauté the onion and garlic in 1 tablespoon oil until soft, about 5 minutes. Add the mushrooms and sauté over medium-high heat, stirring, just until glazed, about 2 minutes. Drain the pasta and place it in a hot serving dish. Toss with the remaining 2 tablespoons oil, lemon juice and zest, mushrooms, parsley, and pepper. Top with spoonfuls of goat cheese and pine nuts and toss again. Serve dusted with grated cheese.

MAKES 2 TO 3 SERVINGS

~ 8 ounces fresh or dried fettuccine

~ 1 small red onion, chopped

~ 1 garlic clove, minced

~ 3 tablespoons extra-virgin olive oil

~ 8 ounces white mushrooms, sliced

~ 1½ tablespoons fresh lemon juice

~ 2 teaspoons grated lemon zest

~ 3 tablespoons minced fresh flat leaf (Italian) parsley

~ Freshly ground black pepper to taste

~ 3 ounces fresh mild white goat cheese at room temperature

~ 3 tablespoons pine nuts, lightly toasted

~ Freshly grated pecorino romano or Parmigiano Reggiano cheese

ENTREES

RACLETTE WITH POTATOES, SAUSAGE, AND FENNEL ~

THIS ALMOST-INSTANT ENTREE CAN DOUBLE AS A FAST

APPETIZER. IN THE ALPINE RESTAURANTS AND BEER HALLS OF SWITZERLAND,

RACLETTE CHEESE IS MELTED OVER AN OPEN FIRE AND ACQUIRES AN INTRIGUING

SMOKY AROMA. IT IS SERVED AS A MEAL WITH BOILED POTATOES, DARK BREAD,

AND CORNICHONS OR OTHER PICKLED VEGETABLES.

~ *12 tiny new potatoes (red, purple, or gold, or a mixture)*

~ *8 ounces raclette, Gruyère, Samsoe, or Jarlsberg cheese*

~ *3 cooked Italian-style sausages or specialty sausages such as chicken-apple (about 12 ounces)*

~ *1 fennel bulb, trimmed and sliced*

~ *12 cornichons or other small pickles*

~ *Dark rye or pumpernickel bread for serving*

Preheat the oven to 350°F. Cook the potatoes in boiling, salted water for 12 to 15 minutes, or until tender when pierced with a fork; drain.

Meanwhile, thinly slice the cheese and place in individual baking dishes or 6-inch ramekins. Place the sausages in a baking dish. Bake the cheese and sausage, at the same time, for about 10 minutes, or until the cheese melts and the sausages are heated through; slice the sausages. Serve the cheese dishes on dinner plates surrounded with the potatoes, sausages, fennel, and pickles, and pass a basket of bread.

MAKES 3 TO 4 SERVINGS

SWISS CHEESE FONDUE ~ THIS CLASSIC DISH IS A HIT FOR A CONVIVIAL WINTER PARTY. YOU CAN MELT THE CHEESE IN A STOVE-TO-TABLE CASSEROLE OVER LOW HEAT ON THE STOVE. ONCE MELTED, BRING IT TO THE TABLE AND PLACE IT OVER A WARMER, SUCH AS A STERNO HEATING UNIT OR ELECTRIC TRAY. OR MELT THE CHEESE IN A CERAMIC CASSEROLE OVER A HEATING UNIT AT THE TABLE. SPEAR THE CRUSTLESS SIDE OF EACH BREAD CUBE WITH A FONDUE FORK, SO THAT THE CRUST GOES INTO THE CHEESE FIRST. IF A MAN'S CUBE SHOULD DROP INTO THE FONDUE, SWISS CUSTOM CALLS FOR HIM TO BUY THE NEXT BOTTLE OF WINE; IF A WOMAN LOSES HER BREAD CUBE, SHE IS SUPPOSED TO KISS HER PARTNER.

Rub the inside of a ceramic fondue pot or stove-to-table casserole with the garlic halves and leave the garlic in the pot. Add the white wine and place over simmering water on low heat on the stove or a heating unit until bubbles form on the surface; do not boil. Toss the cheese with the flour and mustard mixture. Add the cheese to the pot by handfuls, stirring slowly and continuously, and waiting until each handful is completely melted before more is added. Keep stirring until the fondue is thickened and starts bubbling slightly. Stir in the kirsch or other fruit brandy, if desired, and season with nutmeg.

Guests skewer a piece of bread on a fork and swirl it in a figure-eight pattern through the cheese.

MAKES 4 SERVINGS

~ 1 garlic clove, halved

~ 1 3/4 cups Riesling or other fruity dry white wine

~ 8 ounces each (2 cups each) shredded Emmentaler and Gruyère cheese

~ 1 tablespoon flour mixed with 1 teaspoon dry mustard

~ 2 tablespoons kirsch or other fruit brandy (optional)

~ Freshly grated nutmeg to taste

~ 1 French bâtard, cut into 3/4 inch cubes, each with one edge of crust

FOOLPROOF SOUFFLÉ~

THIS REMARKABLY EASY AND QUICK SOUFFLÉ USES WHOLE EGGS BEATEN WITH CREAM, THUS ELIMINATING THE STEP OF SEPARATING THE EGGS. ALTHOUGH IT DOES NOT RISE AS HIGH AS A TRADITIONAL SOUFFLÉ IT HAS A FINE, CREAMY TEXTURE.

~ *4 eggs*

~ *⅔ cup heavy (whipping) cream*

~ *½ teaspoon salt*

~ *Dash of freshly ground black pepper*

~ *⅛ teaspoon each dry mustard and ground nutmeg*

~ *1¼ cups (5 ounces) grated white Cheddar, Gruyère, or Jarlsberg cheese*

~ *⅓ cup grated Parmigiano Reggiano cheese*

Preheat the oven to 425°F. In a large bowl, beat the eggs until fluffy and pale in color. Mix in the cream, salt, pepper, mustard, and nutmeg, beating just until blended. Fold in the cheeses. Pour into a well-buttered 1-quart soufflé dish or baking dish. Bake for 20 to 25 minutes, or until set. Serve at once.

MAKES 4 SERVINGS

SHRIMP AND FETA ~

IN THIS CELEBRATED GREEK SEAFOOD CASSEROLE, OUZO IMBUES THE SHRIMP WITH AN ENTICING ANISE OVERTONE. PILAF IS A PROPER ACCOMPANIMENT ALONG WITH CRUSTY SESAME-COATED BREAD, SLICED VINE-RIPENED TOMATOES, AND MELON WEDGES.

~ 3 tablespoons lemon juice

~ 2 pounds medium raw shrimp, shelled and deveined

~ 1 onion, chopped

~ 1 bunch green onions, white part and some of the green, finely chopped

~ 1 tablespoon olive oil

~ 1 garlic clove, minced

~ 1 can (15 ounces) tomato purée

~ ½ cup dry white wine

~ ½ cup clam juice

~ 2 tablespoons butter

~ 2 tablespoons ouzo or Pernod

~ 1 tablespoon minced fresh oregano, or ¾ teaspoon dried oregano

~ 2 tablespoons minced fresh flat-leaf (Italian) parsley

~ 8 ounces feta cheese, cut into ½ inch pieces

Preheat the oven to 375°F. Pour the lemon juice over the shrimp and let stand while preparing the sauce. In a large saucepan over medium heat, sauté the onions in oil until soft, about 5 minutes. Add the garlic, tomato purée, wine, and clam juice, and simmer, uncovered, for 15 minutes to reduce slightly.

In a large skillet over medium-high heat, sauté the shrimp in the butter until they turn pink, about 4 to 5 minutes. Heat the ouzo or Pernod, ignite, and spoon flaming over the shrimp. Stir the shrimp, oregano, and parsley into the sauce. Spoon into a greased baking dish or individual dishes and scatter the cheese over the top, pushing it in slightly.

Bake in the oven for 15 minutes, or until heated through. Serve at once.

MAKES 6 SERVINGS

CHICKEN BREASTS WITH GOAT CHEESE AND SUN-DRIED TOMATOES ~ THIS ULTRA-FAST,

FESTIVE ENTREE IS EASILY DOUBLED OR TRIPLED FOR UNEXPECTED GUESTS.

Place the chicken breasts in a shallow nonaluminum baking dish or pan. Mix together the mustard, lemon juice, and herbs, and spread over all sides of the chicken; sit at room temperature for 30 minutes. Preheat the oven to 375°F. Bake the chicken for 20 to 25 minutes, or until opaque through-out. Add the tomatoes the last few minutes, just to heat them through. Arrange the chicken breasts on plates, top each with a slice of cheese, and tuck in the arugula leaves.

MAKES 2 SERVINGS

~ *2 split chicken breasts, boned and skinned (about 12 ounces)*

~ *2 tablespoons Dijon or stone-ground mustard*

~ *2 tablespoons fresh lemon juice*

~ *$1\frac{1}{2}$ tablespoons minced mixed fresh herbs such as tarragon, thyme, chives, and flat-leaf (Italian) parsley*

~ *6 drained oil-packed sun-dried tomatoes*

~ *2 ounces fresh mild white goat cheese, cut into 2 slices*

~ *6 to 8 arugula sprigs*

VEAL SALTIMBOCCA ~ CHEESE AND PROSCIUTTO SPIRAL INSIDE NEAT MEAT ROLLS FOR A SUCCULENT GRILLED ENTREE. FOR A SUMMER PARTY, GRILL EGGPLANT SLICES AND RED ONION RINGS AS WELL. WITH A GREEN SALAD STREWN WITH RED AND GOLD CHERRY TOMATOES, CRUSTY COUNTRY BREAD, AND SLICED PEACHES OR NECTARINES STEEPED IN A FRUITY WHITE WINE, A GLORIOUS REPAST IS AT HAND.

~ $1\frac{1}{2}$ pounds thinly sliced veal cutlets, or sirloin tip roast sliced $\frac{3}{16}$ inch thick

~ Salt and freshly ground black pepper to taste

~ 1 tablespoon minced fresh oregano, or $\frac{3}{4}$ teaspoon dried oregano

~ 4 ounces Provolone, Fontina, or Monterey jack cheese

~ 2 ounces thinly sliced prosciutto or ham

~ 2 tablespoons olive oil

~ 1 garlic clove, minced

Pound the meat between 2 sheets of waxed paper until very thin. If using beef, cut it into rectangles about 3 by 5 inches. Sprinkle the meat with salt, pepper, and oregano. Lay a slice of cheese and one of prosciutto or ham on each slice of meat. Roll up from a narrow end. Thread 3 or 4 meat rolls on a skewer. Combine the oil and garlic and brush the mixture over the meat. Grill over medium-hot coals or broil 3 inches from the element of a preheated broiler, turning to brown all sides, for about 8 minutes.

MAKES 4 SERVINGS

BEEF FILLETS WITH GORGONZOLA ~

GORGONZOLA OR ANOTHER CREAMY BLUE CHEESE LIKE DANISH BLUE CASTELLO
GIVES AN ELEGANT FILLIP TO GRILLED STEAK, OR AN UPBEAT TOUCH TO GRILLED
HAMBURGERS.

Place the meat in a self-sealing plastic bag. Mix together the lemon juice, vinegar, oil, and garlic and pour over; seal and marinate 1 to 2 hours at room temperature. Grill the meat over medium-hot coals or under a preheated broiler, turning to brown both sides, about 8 minutes for medium rare. Season with salt and pepper. Transfer to hot plates and dollop with cheese. Garnish with watercress sprigs.

MAKES 2 SERVINGS

~ 2 beef fillets, about 5 ounces each

~ 1 tablespoon fresh lemon juice

~ 2 tablespoons balsamic vinegar

~ 2 tablespoons olive oil

~ 1 garlic clove, minced

~ Salt and freshly ground black pepper to taste

~ 2 ounces Gorgonzola or Danish Blue Castello, at room temperature

~ Watercress sprigs for garnish

grapes

strawberries
Raspberries
apples

Pears
kiwi

DESSERTS

CHEESE ROMANOFF WITH A FRUIT WREATH ~

LIQUEUR ENHANCES CREAMY MASCARPONE OR NATURAL CREAM CHEESE FOR A
FLAVOR-PACKED SPREAD FOR FRUIT OR SWEET BREAD. SWIRL THE CHEESE INTO A
CONE AND WREATH IT WITH BERRIES OR HALVED APRICOTS, COMICE PEAR SLICES,
OR SEEDLESS GRAPES, OR MOLD IT IN A DISH LINED WITH CHEESECLOTH.

~ *8 ounces mascarpone or
natural cream cheese at
room temperature*

~ *2 tablespoons sugar*

~ *2 tablespoons Cointreau,
Grand Marnier, Framboise,
or Amaretto*

~ *2 tablespoons heavy
(whipping) cream*

~ *2 cups fresh fruit such as
strawberries, raspberries,
apricot halves, pear slices,
or seedless grapes*

Place the cheese in a blender, food processor, or mixing
bowl and blend in the sugar, liqueur, and cream until
smooth. Turn out on a serving plate and, with a spatula,
swirl into a cone. Cover and chill until serving time. Or, line
a small heart-shaped mold, charlotte mold, or soufflé dish
with cheesecloth and spoon in the cheese. Cover and chill
several hours. To serve, unmold and ring with fruit.

MAKES 4 SERVINGS

COEUR À LA CRÈME WITH RASPBERRIES ~

VANILLA SUGAR, MADE ONE DAY AHEAD, IMBUES THIS FRENCH CHEESE DESSERT
WITH VANILLA ESSENCE.

Scrape the pulp from the vanilla bean and mix it with the
sugar; place it in a covered jar and let sit for 1 day for the
vanilla to infuse the sugar.

Using dampened cheesecloth, line 6 individual heart
molds with drainage holes or a 4-cup heart basket. Place the
cottage cheese in a blender or food processor and process
until smooth, or push the cheese through a fine-meshed
sieve into a bowl. Mix in the cream cheese and vanilla sugar.
In a deep bowl, whip the cream until soft peaks form. Blend
in the liqueur, if desired, and fold into the cheese mixture
until smooth. Pack into the mold(s), smoothing the top. Fold
the sides of the cheesecloth up over the mixture. Place on a
tray and refrigerate overnight.

To make the raspberry sauce: Puree 1½ cups of the
raspberries in a blender or food processor. Strain the puree
through a fine-meshed sieve into a bowl; discard the seeds.
Stir in the sugar and the optional liqueur. To serve, unmold
the hearts, ring with the berry puree, and garnish with the
remaining raspberries.

MAKES 6 SERVINGS

~ *½ vanilla bean, split
lengthwise*

~ *¼ cup sugar*

~ *1½ cups (12 ounces)
cottage cheese*

~ *8 ounces natural cream
cheese at room
temperature*

~ *½ cup heavy (whipping)
cream*

~ *1 tablespoon framboise
(optional)*

RASPBERRY SAUCE

~ *2 cups fresh or thawed
frozen unsweetened
raspberries*

~ *1 tablespoon sugar*

~ *1 tablespoon framboise
(optional)*

FRUIT AND CHEESE COMBINATIONS

Fruit and cheese are natural partners for a refreshing dessert, snack, or a light meal with bread. Consider mating mellow fruits such as pears, apples, dates, and figs with pungent cheeses like Roquefort, Stilton, ripe Camembert, goat cheese, and aged white Cheddar.

With tart fruits such as strawberries, grapes, kiwifruit, and nectarines, try a mellow cheese such as whole-milk ricotta, Brie, or Teleme, and slightly sweetened or liqueur-flavored mascarpone. With sweet white peaches or nectarines, a triple cream such a Saint-André or Explorateur complements. Because fruits vary in sweetness and acidity, however, there are no firm rules. Apples alone run the spectrum from the supersweet Fuji to acidic early-picked Granny Smiths, making cheese match-ups an ongoing adventure.

Good combinations include:

Fresh pineapple cubes with provolone, Asiago, or Kasseri

Babcock (white) peaches with Saint-André

Comice pears with Gorgonzola or Roquefort

Walnuts, Stilton, and port

Fuji or **Golden Delicious apples** with aged white Cheddar, Jarlsberg, or Gruyère

Strawberries, **blackberries**, **blueberries**, and **raspberries** with natural cream cheese or mascarpone flavored with framboise

Strawberries with peppered Saint-André

Kiwifruit with Explorateur

Papaya with dry jack cheese

Mango with Camembert and Saint-André

Starfruit with fresh mild white goat cheese and a few pistachios

Figs with Gorgonzola or other creamy blue cheese

Dates with Parmagiano Reggiano or Kasseri

Apricots with Saint-André or mascarpone flavored with Cointreau

star fruit

INDEX

TABLE OF EQUIVALENTS

The exact equivalents in the following tables have been rounded for convenience.

US/UK

oz=ounce
lb=pound
in=inch
ft=foot
tbl=tablespoon
fl oz=fluid ounce
qt=quart

Metric

g=gram
kg=kilogram
mm=millimeter
cm=centimeter
ml=milliliter
l=liter

Weights

US/UK	Metric
1 oz	30 g
2 oz	60 g
3 oz	90 g
4 oz (¼ lb)	125 g
5 oz (⅓ lb)	155 g
6 oz	185 g
7 oz	220 g
8 oz (½ lb)	250 g
10 oz	315 g
12 oz (¾ lb)	375 g
14 oz	440 g
16 oz (1 lb)	500 g
1½ lb	750 g
2 lb	1 kg
3 lb	1.5 kg

Oven Temperatures

Fahrenheit	Celsius	Gas
250	120	½
275	140	1
300	150	2
325	60	3
350	180	4
375	90	5
400	200	6
425	220	7
450	230	8
475	240	9
500	260	10